The Contest

Story by Stephen Harrison

Illustrations by Margaret Power

Carl ran toward the high jump and leaped over the bar. As he landed on the mat, he knew that he had jumped much higher than anyone else in his class.

"That was the best jump so far!" said his friend Shaun. "You're going to be the champ again this year."

"Yes, I think I am," replied Carl. "No one at school can jump that high."

Mrs. Taylor called to the boy who was last to have his turn. His name was Michael, and he had only just come to Fairfield School. Shaun and Carl watched as he stood up and stared at the bar for a few moments.

3

Very slowly, the new boy raised himself up on his toes and took a deep breath. Then he approached the bar with several long strides, and leaped over it easily.

"Wow!" said Shaun. "Did you see that, Carl? He jumped as high as you did!"

"That was excellent, Michael!" said Mrs. Taylor. "It's obvious that you've done the high jump before!"

Michael grinned. "I was the champ at my last school," he replied.

Carl began to feel worried. He had been expecting to win easily, but now he would have to compete against Michael.

And the bar would be raised ...

Carl stood and looked at the bar. Suddenly, it seemed very high. He ran up to it and, as he went over, he hit it with his foot. He could hear the bar clattering to the ground as he landed on the mat.

Michael had his turn next. Over he went, and everybody clapped. Then Carl knocked the bar off twice in a row. As it fell down after his final attempt, he knew that he was out of the contest. Michael was the new champion.

Carl was very disappointed. He sat down beside Shaun and said, "I'm not going to do the high jump any more."

"But you're really good at it," said Shaun. "You can't give up, just like that. Why don't you come to the gym with me tomorrow, and do some training?"

Shaun was good at running, and every Saturday morning he went to the Westside Athletics Club, where his father was a coach. He had been trying to get Carl to join, but Carl wasn't interested. "Training is boring," he said.

The next day was Saturday, and Carl went to watch a local soccer game with his father. As they walked up and down the sideline, Carl noticed some children jogging around a track in the park next door.

He wandered over to have a closer look, and realized that one of the children was Shaun. "Hi, Shaun!" he shouted. "What are you doing?"

"This is the Westside Athletics Club!" answered Shaun. "Why don't you come and have a look around?"

"Okay!" said Carl. "I'll just tell Dad where I'm going."

Shaun took Carl over to the high-jump area, where his father was coaching some children. Carl noticed that they had a different way of jumping over the bar. Instead of going feet first, as he did, they went over backward, leading with their head and shoulders.

Carl asked Shaun's father to teach him how to do this style of jumping, and then he practiced with the other children. Carl soon realized that he was able to jump much higher than before, and he began to enjoy himself.

The following week, Carl joined the Westside Athletics Club and, every Saturday, he trained with the other children.

By the end of the season, Carl was the best high jumper in his age group, and he was looking forward to the annual contest with the Eastside Athletics Club.

On the day of the contest, everyone went to welcome the Eastside children. As Carl watched them coming through the gate, he groaned. "Look who's here!" he said to Shaun.

"It's Michael!" said Shaun.

"And I'll have to jump against him, because we're the same age," said Carl. "I haven't got a chance now."

"Of course you have," said Shaun's father. "You just need to concentrate, and remember everything you've learned during the season."

The two boys walked over to meet Michael. "Hi!" said Carl. "Come with us, and we'll show you where the high jump is."

Michael grinned. "Okay," he said.

The contest started, and Carl and Michael took turns to jump. After a while, Carl realized that he was jumping as well as Michael, and he began to grow more confident.

Then Michael failed two jumps in a row. And on his final attempt, the bar wobbled ... and fell down after him.

"This is my chance now," said Carl to himself. "I only have to clear this height, and I've won!" But he knew that the bar was higher than he had ever jumped before.

Carl took a deep breath, and began his run-up. He leaped high into the air but, as he went over, he felt his heel touch the bar. He landed on the mat and turned to look back. The bar was shuddering. Carl sat very still, staring at it.

For several moments, the bar looked as if it might fall. Then it slowly stopped moving and stayed where it was.

Everyone cheered, and Carl leaped off the mat with his hands in the air. He had won the contest!